DREAM GARDEN

POEMS

by

Ayin Weaver

NOVELWEAVER PRESS

DREAM GARDEN, Poems
© 2023, Ayin Weaver /N. Reimer

ISBN: 978-09742339-5-6

Cover art: *Lucy's Garden,*
by Nina Reimer; www.artflare.net
Interior art: by Nina Reimer

Book design: Jo-Anne Rosen

Published by
NovelWeaver Press
novelweaverpress@usa.net

Manufactured in the USA
First edition, 2023

In memory
of my mother
&
For my beloved creative family & friends

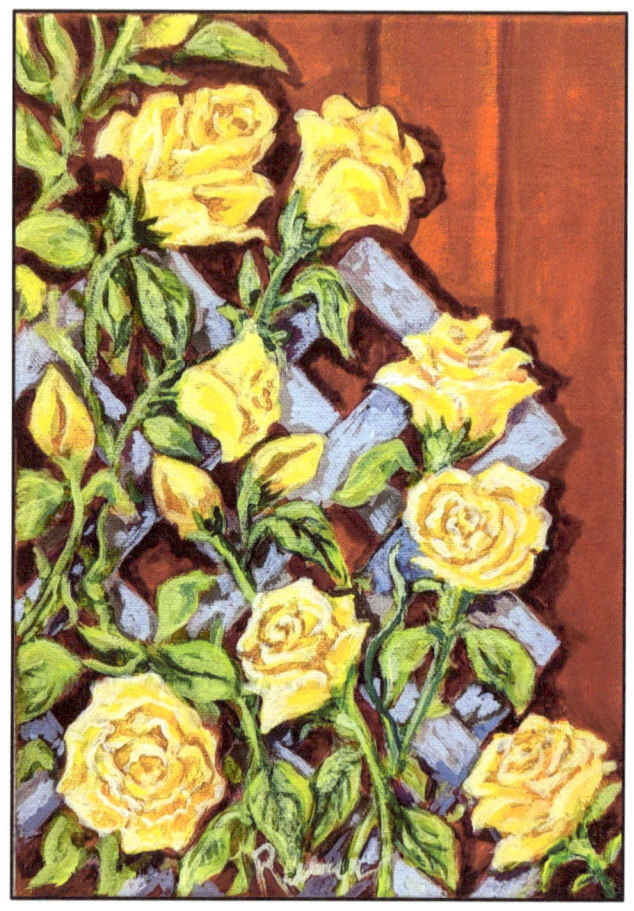

My Summer Roses, acrylic on canvas   N. Reimer

Contents

I Didn't Know

I didn't know I'd love the land
Of dry air, cactus and Mesquite
Until I lived beneath the blooming Palo Verde
Of my first desert spring and bathed
In red and purple light of the sun's smile
Upon skyward Catalina peeks that stood majestic
In view from my veranda

I didn't know love as the company
Of reptiles big and small, striped lizards
That came each morning to do push-ups
Sun-bathing on warm rocks along-side my porch
While I leisurely sipped my breakfast tea
And drank in the cool morning air
As doves made nests in adjacent Acacia trees
Cooing their simple love-songs, softly

I didn't know love as exaltation
Under the black night sky, a blanket of stars
So clear and plenty, as if within reach
Except when the moon rose huge
Over the mountain top, illuminating a skyline
Of tall Saguaro, night creatures strange and wild
King snake and diamondbacks, new to me
Javalina, cat squirrels, not in books I'd read
Only scorpion, bobcat, coyote—familiar then

I didn't know love as dizziness
From sweet fragrance, an oasis of blossoms
The second spring, when swarms of bees
Hundreds strong, hummed in flowering orange trees
Their collective rhythm vibrating, pulsating
Accented by the red cardinals' serenade
While pink Lantana flirted with blue butterflies
Prickly pear displayed juicy fuchsia buds
Tobacco trees' gold swirls lured hummingbirds
And quail scurried, young ones in perfect rows

I didn't know I'd fall in love
With Desert's rain, cold nights, warm arid days
She crept toward me quietly, like a mountain lion
Wrapped her cunning ways around me, her beauty
Seducing me, like a voluptuous lover
Beckoning me with her coy white-tail rabbits
Enchanting me with her owl calls at dusk
Bewitching me with her hot breath, flaming sunsets
Enticing me with her whispering wind-swept sands
Into her vast and ancient ocean bed,
Where I could hear the song of my soul again

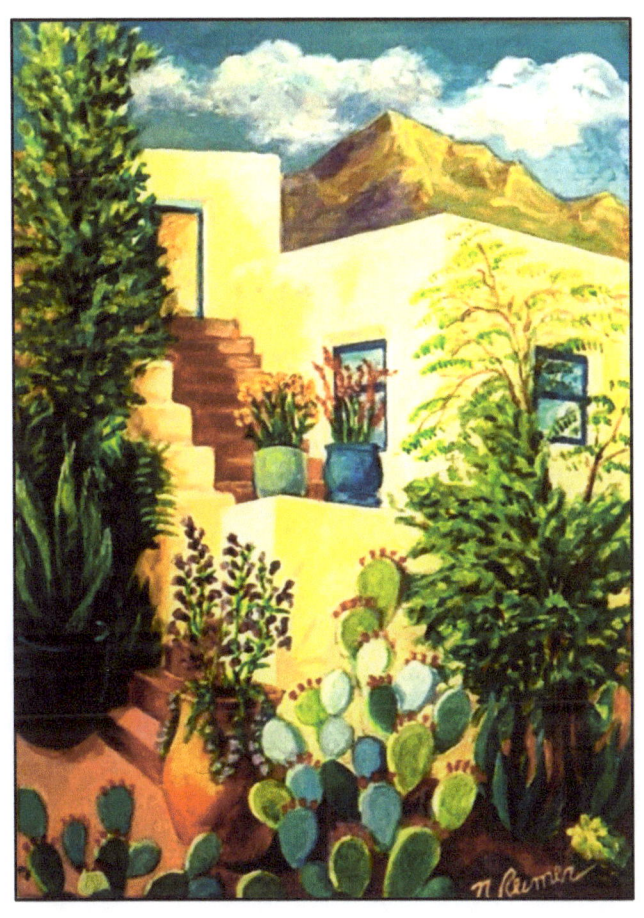

Remembering El Dia de los Muertos

A Shaman remembers for others,
Remembers for those who cannot,
Like me and my elephant spirits,
My whale companions, the lot

I carry the ancient memories,
To those who seek me out,
My job is to speak with the ancestors,
Some whisper, some sing and some shout

I remember those missed by the living,
I recall the events of their lives,
I share in my own way, a message,
That brings tears, laughter and sighs

I remember for Bertha, her grandmother,
A women of nickels and love,
I remember for Paul, his mother,
Her faith in the heavens above

I remember for Jim, his uncle,
A man of violin duets and berets,
I remember for Steve, his grandfather,
His laughter, cigars and wise ways

I remember for Edna, her Godmother,
A woman of needles and thread,
I remember for Sara, her mother,
By her own hand found her when dead

I remember for Nakisha and Andy,
For Nathan, Sophia and Grace,
Their ancestors longing to speak out,
Of yet another time and place

Being one who remembers for others,
My ancestors also come through,
They speak to me always at night-time,
Of memories both happy and blue

I remember my tomb in Egypt,
A gold-laden treasured affair,
I remember my boyhood in forests,
Of streams of clear water and air

I remember the first war in Europe,
And the soldiers who killed us all,
I remember the horse on the battlefield,
The one who survived Custer's fall

I remember my five dark-eyed children,
Doing cleaning for rich folks all day,
I remember bedding with strangers,
Brothel's loveless rolls in the hay

I remember leaving wife and daughter,
On a long walk, a trail of tears,
I remember my inventor husband,
Whose dark skin meant no credit or cheers

I remember the statues of Buddha,
Bathing the deities sacred and still,
I remember a voyage by ocean,
Of enslavement and torture to kill

I remember the boats on the blue sea,
Sailing 'long the Isle of Lesbos,
And the graceful song of my lover,
From sweet songs that now bring us close

I remember my father's old bookstore,
Closing when the day was done,
I remember a young man, his music,
Who now enriches my life like the sun

But most of all I remember,
That we are all passing through,
What's important in remembering,
Is the PEACE from remembering you

When I look at you, I can see me,
As we were in a lifetime gone by,
We're all one, please try to remember,
Ancestors of one of kind—a lie

So remember though life is but transient,
And we have all met here before,
We must care for the Earth in our time here,
Like our Ancestors returning once more

So, welcome to all of my Ancestors,
Black, brown, yellow, white, and red,
Welcome my Ancestors of all Faiths,
As we celebrate *The Day of the Dead*

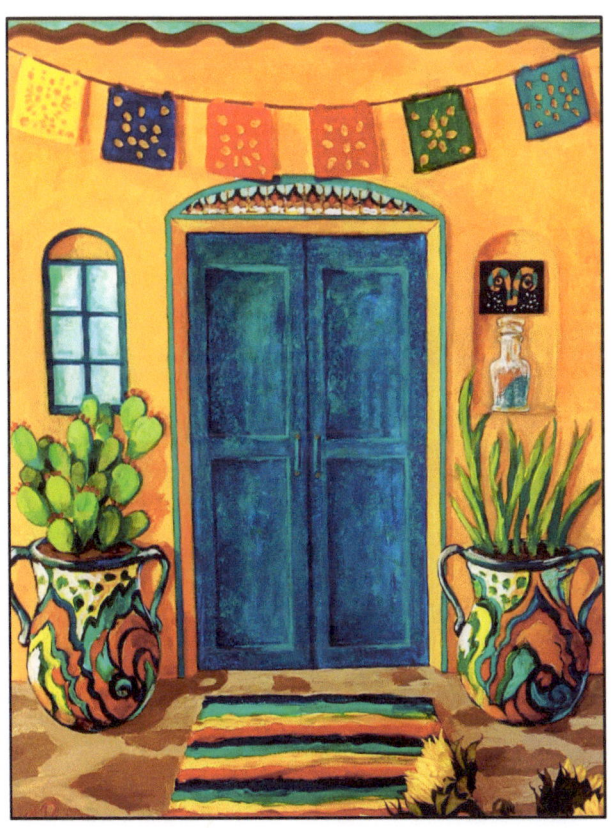

Mi Casa, Su Casa, acrylic on canvas   *N. Reimer*

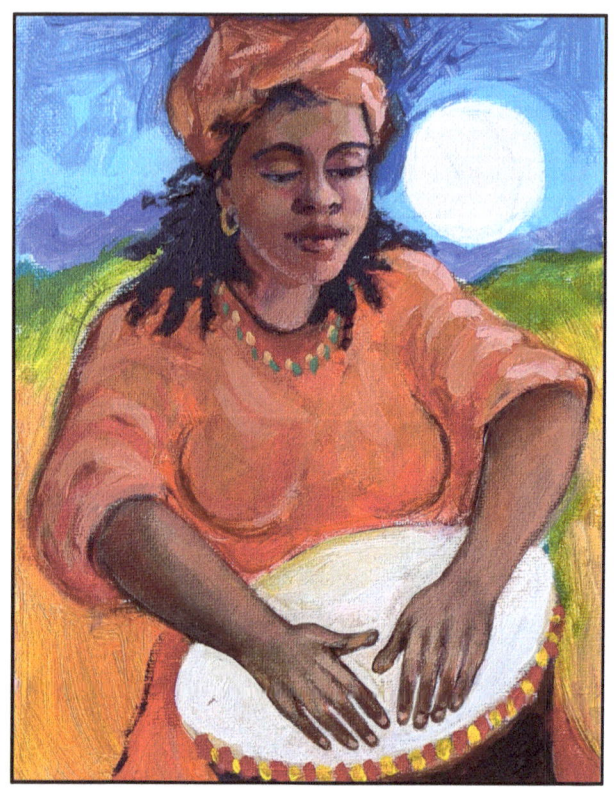

Drumming Dreamtime, acrylic on canvas   *N. Reimer*

Ode to Rhythm and Rhyme

They say a serious poet doesn't rhyme,
Not addicted to beat or time,
Never interested in whimsy or song.
They say a serious poet's words belong,
Each syllable placed with emphasis strong.
They say a proper poet's words do heed
The rules of an elite and esoteric breed,
Like philosophers that great minds read,
Where words are power unto themselves,
Every nuance, style into which one delves.

They say the rhyming poet's words are trite
And flimsy just to hold the course,
Not sophisticated, but more a loss
For words that vibrate and resound,
They're simply redundant or repetition bound.
They say only serious poets win awards
For heartfelt stanzas deep accords.
How can one rhyme about pain and dying,
Serious subjects defiled in flaky fair--
Words of rhyme have no business there.

But lots of great poets have taken to rhyming.
So say the ancestors of diva, Carmen McCray,
Whose many song poems that from her day
Begin with a sweet, slow, mellow refrain,
Made our hearts ache, yearn, again and again.
What of Dylan, Fitzgerald, Lennon and others?
And song poet Marley, the great Jamaican brother?
From ancient chants, lullabies of grandmothers,
Flutes sing, drums beat, rhyming poets give birth
To some of the greatest music on planet earth.

What of Frost, Longfellow, Dickenson, Milay?
Or has memory of them just slipped away?
Were their poems so fancy free,
One could not detect depth or earnest intent
To portray life's struggles, substance, content?
So, let's hear it for poets that love to rhyme,
For songwriters and children stepping in time
To the beat of drums, and words that roll quickly
Off the tips of tongues and fingers that write,
Just like serious poets--late into the night.

Blackberries for Olie

We walk at summer sunset
Along the winding dirt road
Redwoods soar into a cloudless sky
The sun pokes its brilliant rays
Between the tall branches
The heat of the day
Cools into just right for walking
And picking blackberries still warm
Wild, abundant wherever I look

At the edges of the road they wait
Enticing me, my mouth waters
With the slightest nudge, a plump berry
Dark and firm—yet soft, succumbs
To my nimble fingers' gentle pull
Falling into my eager hands
Into my glass jar for safe-keeping
They land one upon the other
Except for one, I hold to the light

I examine its sparkling richness
Tantalizing my little dog
Who stands momentarily still
Looking at me in anticipation
His eyes riveted to the slightest move
Of my hand, my intent he intuits
Opening his mouth at the instant
I drop the luscious berry down, down
As if we have rehearsed this act

His timing is perfection in motion
But he does not chew, does not savor
The juicy sweetness, he swallows
Looks up for a repeat performance
I pick a ripe blackberry from the vine
For myself to satisfy, taste its honey
I press tongue to palette, dwell in its
Liquid essence, all my senses
Transformed by the bounty of berries

I, a city dweller, turned country girl
Luxuriate in a summer walk along
A country road with my companion
Breathing redwood and eucalyptus
As the wildflowers entice honeybees
Woodpeckers, songbirds tap and sing
In harmonic balance amidst the breeze
The blackberries beckon us
We walk and happily comply

What could be more delightful than this?

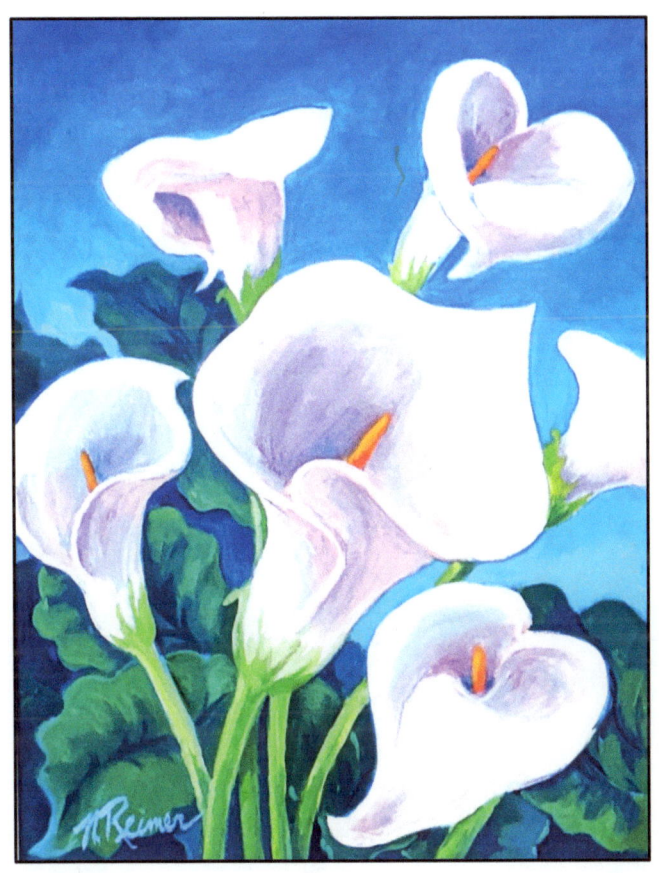

Calla Lily II, acrylic on canvas   *N. Reimer*

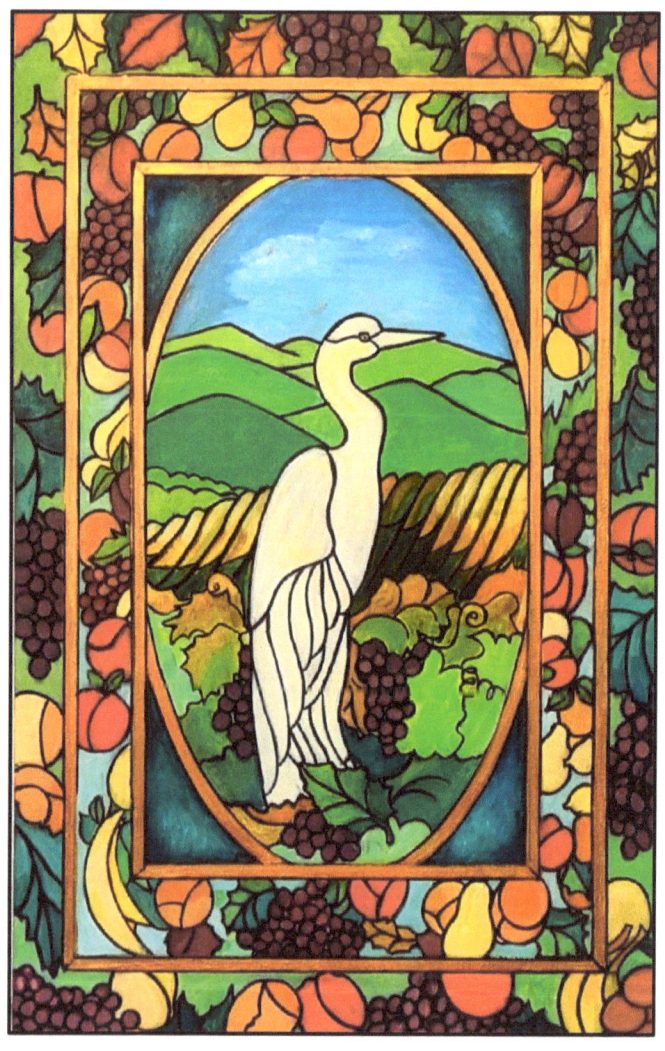

Abundance, acrylic on canvas   *N. Reimer*

Autumn

Vineyards of golden orange and red
The sky as blue as blue
I think of you as days cool down
Toward winter months anew

I say a little prayer for you
That you are happy then
Safe and loved, and for us in turn
That we may laugh again

Women's Hands

Our hands have seen the light of day
From mountain tops and canyon bay
We've touched the dark of night, as well
From Ravens' flight to Danger's smell
We've seen the world from others' eyes
From every color, shape and size

Women's hands have birthed the smallest babe
Cradled the dying in life's shade
We've touched the girl who survived the lies
And heartbreak in a boy's final good-byes
Our hands have touched the child at play
Then witnessed joy just stripped away

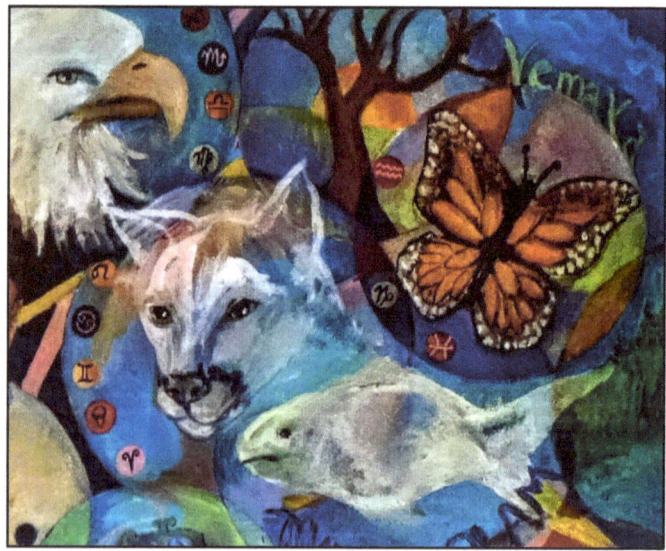

Tikkun Olam (detail), acrylic on canvas   *N. Reimer*

Women's hands have touched the ocean blue
Whales, dolphin, fish, sea lions too
We've touched mighty forests in the sun
Sustaining life to breathe and run
Our hands have driven past logging trucks
Cleaned deadly oil from gulls and ducks

Our hands have touched a thousand souls
Whose hearts yearn for the comforting folds
Of a long forgotten place and time
Where beauty, love, simply thrived sublime
Healing hands that touch, can see the light
That heals the body in its darkest fight

Women's hands that heal, vanquish the dark
We soothe the pain, replenish the spark
Of Spirit yearning to be free
Desire ingrained in you and me
Our hands that see and heal to start
Remove the fear and open the heart

We join hands to heal, caress the land
And all the creatures small and grand
Gorillas, elephants, bees and bats
Deer, bear and wolf, all dogs and cats
The birds with whom our hearts do soar
The tiny sand crab on the shore

All hands that see and heal the heart
Will not allow beauty to be torn apart
Our healing hands must write, create
Spread Love and Peace to seal our fate
With our healing hands, we must give birth
Embrace women's work of saving Earth!

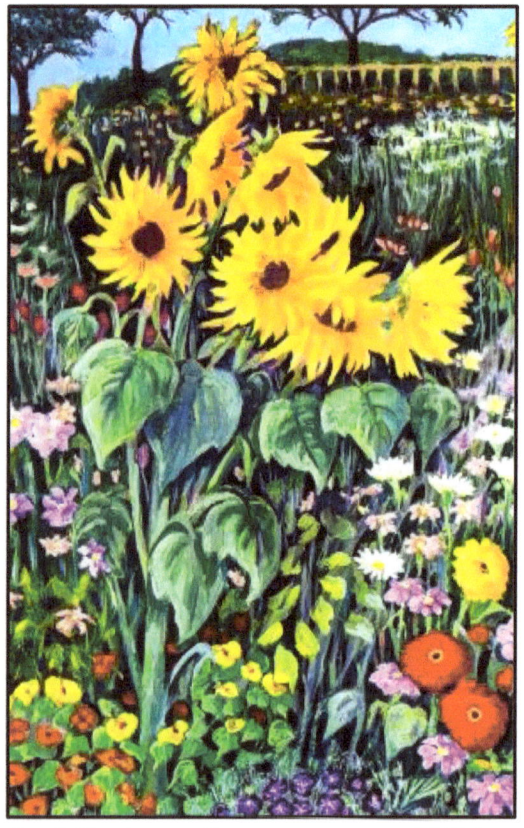

Lucy's Garden, acrylic on canvas　　　*N. Reimer*

Mother Took Me to See the King

At two in the morning she woke me from bed
Time to see history in the making she said
With a whisper, a nudge, we were out in a flash
And soon on the train and off in a dash

I was young and excited to be going away
With Mother to be seeing the King on this day
Still dark and cool in the morning twilight
The humidity, heat grew with every new sight.

Passed buses upon buses, miles they did drive
Was the whole world to see the Great One arrive?
We got off the train in the blistering heat
With thousands of other folks walking the street

Chanting and singing and praising this day
Freedom's call heard, there was no other way
I was eager to hear and see Freedom ring
To see the great city, but especially the King

Crowds so massive, I couldn't see where they led
So I left mother with friends and ran up ahead
Suddenly a less crowded place at the end
I looked up to see some great stairs to ascend

At top, the podium, stood the one we would hear
The man they called King, full of love, not of fear
Being young and wild with passion and daring
I climbed a statue for better seeing and hearing

I turned my head for a glance you might say
What I saw remains etched in my heart to this day
The masses of people, the heat not withstanding
Stood shoulder to shoulder, freedom demanding

Their cheers and their shouts as true and clear
As the blue skies above, for the whole world to hear
The love and the power spread out like a wave
Covering every inch from horizon to stage

The pools of blue water stood reflecting the sky
The only place people did not occupy
Then a voice rang out, so strong and so loud
As if heaven itself had enchanted the crowd

The voice of the King dreaming and inspiring
A vision he painted, our hearts yearning, desiring
He fed us and nurtured us with courage and grace
His passion contagious on every face

Like cool water flowing into parched land
We all stood together each holding a hand
Then we sang, we cried, we hugged and we cheered
We made promises to God, we no longer feared

We'd overcome and stand up when it counted
Fight injustice and racism where ever it mounted
He dreamed a dream, the King did that day
It was history that would begin to pave the way

And no one who heard him was ever the same
Not my mother nor I, would forget that refrain
My mother took me to see the King
In August of 63, I was only a teen

Now many years later, peace and justice still deem
That we keep on marching and dreaming the dream!

A Tightly Woven Rug

We were once a tightly woven rug
Inseparable at first
I held your small body close to mine
Wrapped in love and kisses
Now your grown and gone your way
I let go, but always my heart misses

We were once a tightly woven rug
I hoped and dreamed like mothers do
I'd be your rock, let nothing hurt you
Wrapped in love and kisses
Now your grown and gone your way
I let go, but always my heart misses

We were once a tightly woven rug
But over time the threads did part
Naturally growing, going on your way
Now Love and kisses from far away
Still close to my heart you'll always stay
Our bond weaves through time eternal

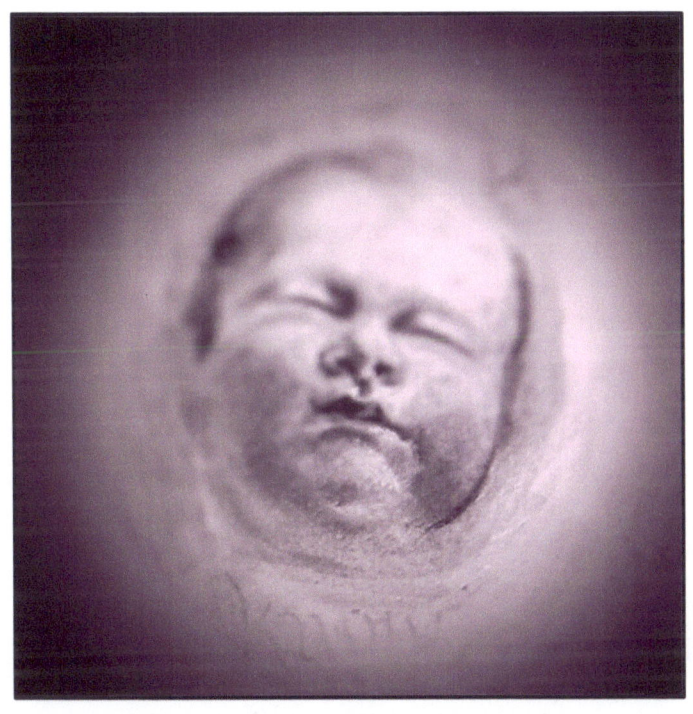

My Beloved Boy (Tikkun Olam detail), acrylic on canvas
N. Reimer

Lean Years

Song to My Child

When the cupboards were almost empty
When panic replaced food and plenty
Like a tidal wave of guilt and despair
When there was no breath, no fresh air
The thought of you held me fast to the Light

When loneliness clouded my view
When desperation came anew
When nothing seemed to go as planned
If anger sparked, if flames were fanned
The thought of you held me fast to the Light

When sorrow and regret did abound
Within the four walls, I felt drowned
If only I had done this or that about
Trying to rise above the doubt
The thought of you held me fast to the Light

When I found I could take no more
My hope lost by another closed door
When exhaustion overtook my day
And the aches and pains wouldn't go away
The thought of you held me fast to the Light

Now when day is done, as nighttime falls
The calm of evening from workday's squalls
Your sweet smile, your sparkling eyes
Your voice so strong, your words so wise
Hold my heart fast to the Light of Love

Lilacs for Mother

Lilacs beckoned me in the dewy dawn of spring,
Alluring fragrance blowing thru my bedroom window,
Enticing me outdoors.
Voluptuous purple petals and light lavender—
Awakening my senses, my joy.

Lilacs, my mother's favorite flower too
Cutting blooming branches, the fullest ones for her
I kept a glass vase overflowing,
Purple plumes on kitchen's window sill—
Because, I knew it pleased her.

In time, cut lilacs faded, crisp and drab
Searching bushes, last buds hiding among leaves
To see her smile, breathe in sweet ambrosia,
Until there was no more—
Like the season, a bond short-lived.

Then early velvet roses clung to vines
Offering themselves, aromatic petals sweetening air,
I let them linger along the garden fence
Whispering my promise—
To pick the choicest ones in summer.

In the hottest season's sun, I'd come.
Snare the big ones, yellow and red, that she'd admire,
Knowing her frugality, no cost for nature's bounty
Unlike five and dime presents—
Of lipstick and perfume, she'd scoff.

When cool autumn breezes blew, I watched
Roses fade like memories, petals scatter in the wind,
Then fallen autumn leaves, dazzling colors ablaze
Pressed in wax paper place mats—
To brighten her plate at dinner time.

Before the snow, I rummaged for nickels and dimes,
Hard pressed to buy chocolate coins and oranges,
Lit Menorah candles for tradition sake alone,
For a smile at holiday time—
A reflection, like a twinkle in her eye.

Then I dreamed of spring anew, when
Lilacs would bloom again, sweet fragrance floating
Through my bedroom window, aroma adrift
Evoking visions of a purple bouquet—
As soft as a mother's kiss.

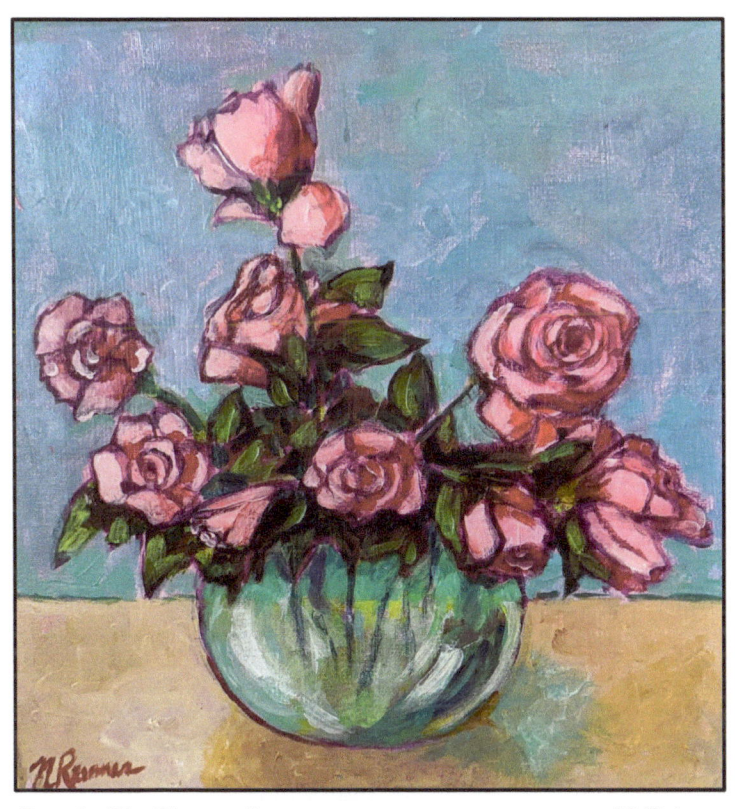

Roses in Blue Vase acrylic on canvas   *N. Reimer*

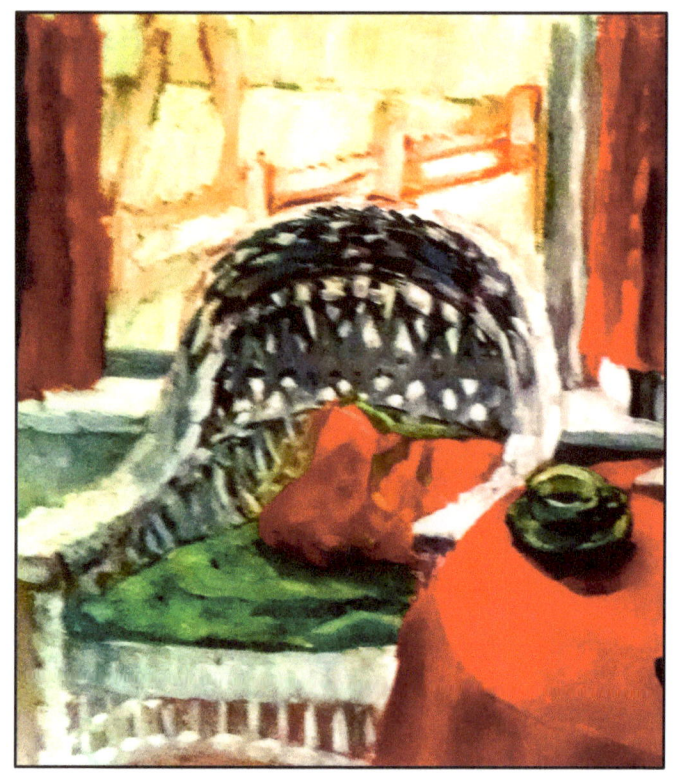

Winter Comfort, oil on canvas   *N. Reimer*

Passion

The chair did not matter
Soft or hard, metal or wood
As long as the typewriter worked
She would sit long hours

The chair did not matter
As long as grandmother made dinner
Father came home on time
We did our homework

The chair did not matter
As long as the dishes were done
Teeth brushed, bedtime came at nine
And the place was quiet

The chair did not matter
As long as the typewriter worked
On the long kitchen table
Her papers and books stacked neatly

The chair did not matter to mother
Her ninety words a minute
Spilled out from a passion
We watched but did not understand

The chair does not matter
Soft or hard, metal or wood
As long as my computer works
Now I, like her, can sit long hours

Flying With Angels

Off the roof I leaped
And flew without stops
Soaring like a bird
Out over treetops

The angels guided me
Held me safe in their wings
Voices of softness
Were whispering things

"It's okay now," they said.
"You need not despair.
Grandmother is here now.
She's as light as the air."

I woke up on the rooftop
Teetering at the edge
Grandmother was gone and
I leaped from the ledge

Her death had enraged me
The cruelty and guilt
No one spoke to me either
So my anguish just built

Abandoned and alone
They had cut off her hair
My parents were silent
They didn't seem to care

Her long locks I'd braided
Night after night
Then we'd climb into bed
And turn out the light

She'd tell me stories
Of when she was a girl
Of her life and her dreams
As my mind it would swirl

We had been together
Since I had been born
Now she lay in a coffin
Like a bride all adorned

I slept in her big bed
That night all alone
The sun rose the next morning
I tried to lay prone

I reached for my blanket
But it was not at my feet
I opened my eyes
Waking up not complete

I squinted, then gasped
As I looked at the ground
From the edge of the roof
I was barely earth bound

I'd been light as feather
With angels I flew
Out over the treetops
My grandmother knew

The angels had guided me
Held me safe in their wings
Voices of softness
Kept whispering things

"It's okay" they said gently
"You need not despair
Grandmother is here now
She's as light as the air

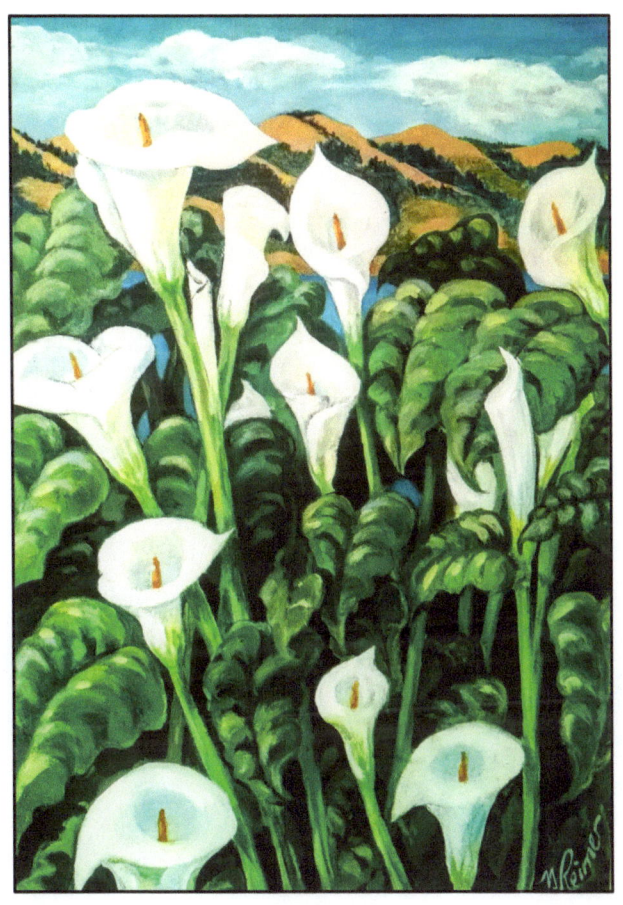

Calla Lily Dreams, oil on canvas   *N. Reimer*

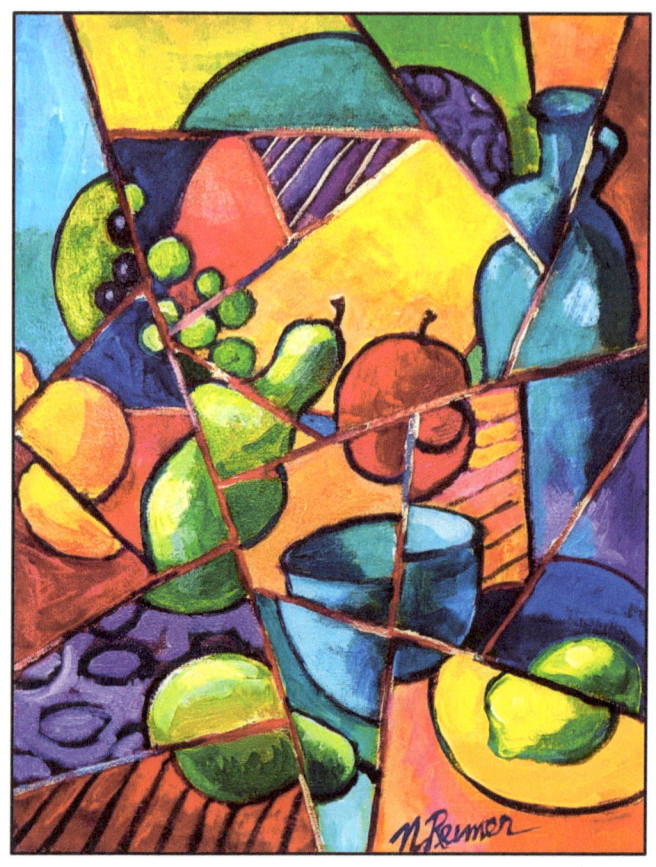

Essentials, acrylic on canvas   *N. Reimer*

If Only

If only, I had played those lottery numbers
I scribbled in my notebook, but did not use,
I could have written to my heart's desire
The books and poems that lay half-completed,
Waiting for stolen moments, late at night.

If only, I could've turned back time,
Found a place where artists mattered,
Where art was not squeezed into hours stolen,
And essentials available to know peace of mind
Where sacrifice was occasional, not the daily norm.

If only, I had a room of my own to sit and paint,
Not shared with siblings, lovers or children,
But a separate space for unburdened, guilt-free time
To create the expression of my soul's desire,
Grateful for every moment of such freedom.

But then again, I may have never known the stories
Of courage, survival, the kindness of strangers,
The frailty and healing of a broken heart,
Or a spirit aflame with inspiration, creative fire,
Devotion to a passion that knows no room or place.

Now, whether my dreams arrive tomorrow or not,
Days end will find me channeling my muse's song,
Busy with paints and pages, editing each new line,
Until dawn climbs over country hills or cityscapes,
Wherever I may room or roam—

Writing and painting, until my final journey home.

Dawn Breaks

At the crack of dawn, a woodpecker woke me
Sounding like a jackhammer against the wall
But now the sun has reached high noon
Hundreds of voices trilling, tweeting
Singing under the bright desert sky
Hummers, quail, and morning doves
An endless chatter of chores and news
Everyone has a story to tell

The birds rouse me from my grieving bed
Where I lay for longer than I should
Filled with sadness of my own heart's story
Still unhealed, dream-shattered by betrayal
Broken promises of forever and always
A heart that cries itself to sleep, barely sleeps
At night, when birds rest for morning songs
And you are still out dancing.

Twisting the truth until it grins
Deceit concealed behind a soft voice
Lulling my heartstrings to sleep
While you lay in the arms of another
Mixed messages short-circuiting my synapses
Soul's deep bonds of trust, breaking after
Reuniting our love song, our passion
Coming home to find another in my place

Now sorrow-filled memories I breathe
Trying forgiveness through the forest
Of I will always love you, blown kisses
What's past is past, you say, not enduring pain
Moving on is the new refrain,
The song you sing at the break of dawn
As my heart lies beneath a lake of tears
Like monsoon rain drowning dry river beds

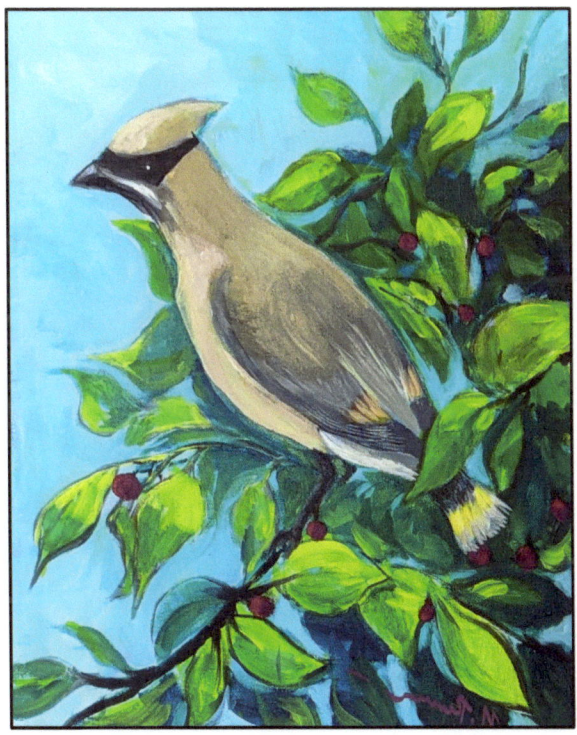

Morning Song, acrylic on canvas   *N. Reimer*

Where Does the Love Go?

Where does the love go
After we part in despair
Does it just dissipate into the air
Into the next dimension or time
And simply continue on, sublime
Where does the love go?

Where does the love go
That was once so strong
Held us together, thru rain or storm
That no matter what, it still shined
Does it exist anywhere in form or kind
Where does the love go?

Where does the love go?
Does it just fade away
Evaporating in the heat of the day
How can it turn itself inside out
Suddenly one day, it's not about
Where does the love go?

Where does the love go?
Does it have its own fate
Does it journey onward to create
Rainbows of joy, new love to grow
Birth of new lovers, like seeds do sew
Where does the love go?

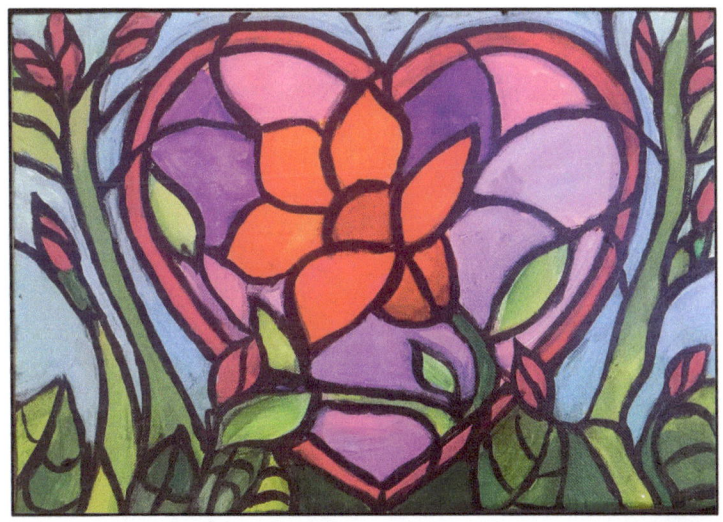

From the Heart, acrylic on canvas *N. Reimer*

Where does the love go?
Does it sleep, dream at night
Unaffected by quarrels and spite
Transformed by cosmic energy
Join other souls who are meant to be
Where does the love go?

Does anyone know?

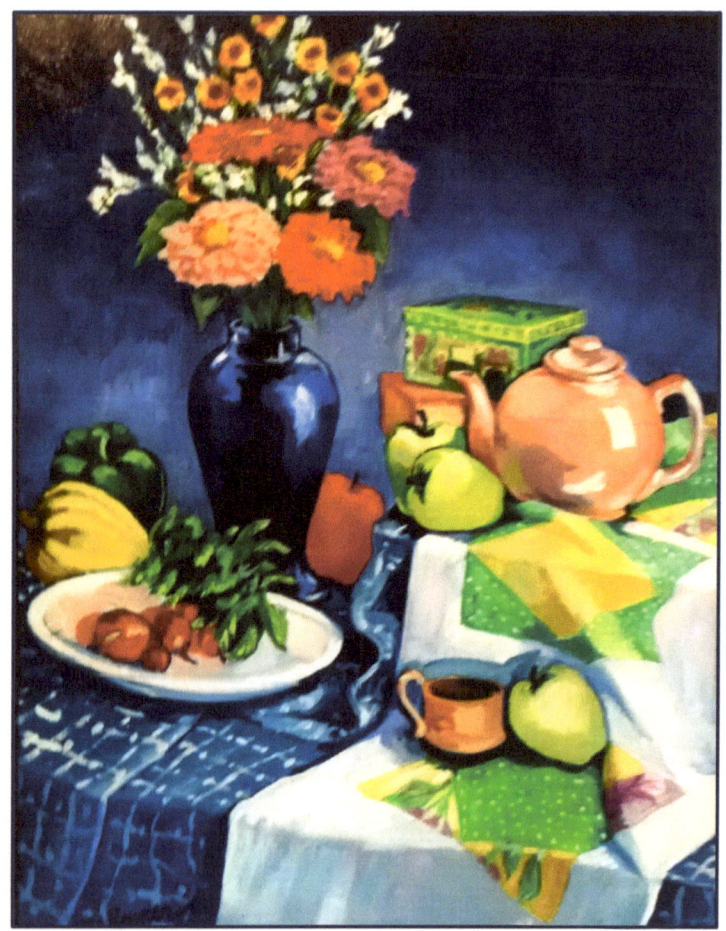

Tea Time, oil on canvas   N. Keimer

The Storyteller

I came with broken wings
And a heart torn asunder
By a poison arrow, betrayed of a lover
I could not fly, barely speak or eat
The fabric of my soul lay tattered at my feet

She took me in and wrapped me long
In the white light of stories and heart song
Mending my spirit with cosmic gold thread
She coaxed me with wine, sweet fruit and bread
By the sea waves lullaby and a warm feathered bed

I came with broken wings and heart
She soothed my mind, which had come apart
With her ancient wisdom and common sense
An ear of kindness, her listening intense
She drowned my sorrow with humor's defense

She pulled me from darkness far along
With a healer's heart and a spirit strong
By her flower-filled garden of fragrant smell
She gave me safe harbor, her own stories did tell
Illuminating my path, 'till I no longer fell

I came with broken wings and heart so cold
By the hearth, with hot tea and divine stories of old
She pulled me to life, transformed my condition
Wings healed by the Storyteller, a soulful Magician
A better friend, one couldn't find anywhere

Olive, healer, storyteller—extraordinaire!

Bess McCray at 86

Bess McCray is 86
Sits with legs apart
In jeans and hiking boots
Lamenting her dead gold fish
Lost in the fire that took her place
From candle burning cocoon to
Inferno devouring her belongings
Artwork, journals, and plants

Bess McCray at 86
Swatted the flames
With bed clothes that fed the fire
Sprayed water from the kitchen sink
To no avail but determined
On her own to put out the fire
Called her daughter but not 911
At last a neighbor did

Bess at 86, lost her possessions
Her beloved books and those
That belonged to the library
Her family comes to help her out
She waits for her home to be fixed
Returned to its former state
While she decorates a temporary place
Feels displaced, disoriented, but laughs

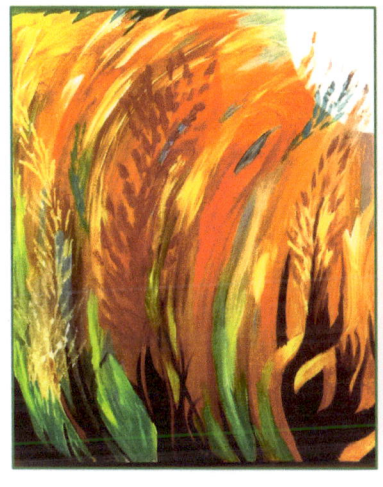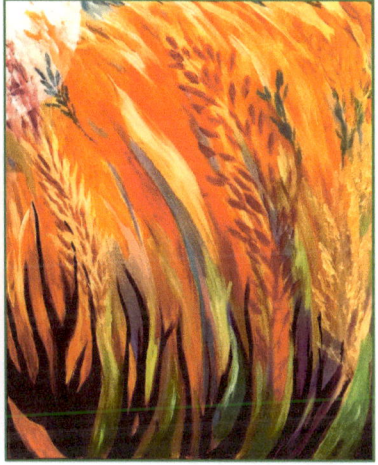

Moon Fire, acrylic on canvas   *N. Reimer*

Bess Mc Cray is 86
She sits with legs apart in
Her jeans and hiking boots
Her wide wrinkled hands on knees
Hands of a sculptor not dainty or meek
Hands of wife once, mother of five
Grandmother, Great Grandmother
Laments a life of solid memories lost

Bess Mc Cray is 86
Must mean something, she says
Heart aching as her pacemaker
Keeps time and the artist's hope alive
Environmental artist, clay woman hands
Pit fire woman, clay and fire together
Raku rattles in bonfires on the beach
Her creative fire still ablaze within

Bess Mc Cray still smiles at 86
A new beginning, I guess, she says
In her jeans and hiking boots
In a healing circle of strong women
Sends healing to the earth, its oceans
And eyes the fire star in the heavens
Worries about global warming and
The great white bears of polar North

Bess Mc Cray is 86
She sits, defiant, strong hands on knees
An Earth Goddess! Earth Healer!
Fire Warrior! Woman of Fire!
Out of the ashes, she survives to find
Her family stronger, friends warmer,
Laughter heartfelt, longer...and
Marvel and meaning still, in everything!

If Ever There Would Come a Day

If ever there would come a day
When artists ruled the world
The streets would be ablaze in colors
Flags would be unfurled

Creativity would flourish
In schools across the land
Teachers would be paid their due
Different drummers for the band

If ever there would come a day
When woman ruled the earth
Streets would be alive with song
Children would come first

No war, no bombs or devastation
Of homes, forests, land or sea
Food and medicine abundant
People, the first priority

If ever there would come a day
That we all understood
There is no place to run and hide
Earth is our neighborhood

The air we breathe, the seas and lakes
The plants and soil devine
Can't continue to be destroyed
Mother Earth is on the line

There will certainly come a day
Present time becomes the past
Earth will make a rapid shift
Transformation comes at last

Thrift

The clothes I loved
My thrift store specials
Began to live—to breathe, to talk,
Until, I could not bare their stories

Cowboy shirts with shiny snaps,
Well-worn, tight boys' button jeans,
Finely crafted vests with pockets
Belts and boots of soft leather

Their sad and lonely stories
Followed me out the door each day
I looked by all accounts alone,
But he or she or they were with me—

On my back, pressed close to my skin,
Wrapped a dying breath, long-lost love,
Or some angry torrent around me
Begged for my constant attention

Their aesthetic, color, style I missed
But I put my thrift store threads away
Thirty years since strangers' clothes
Have touched my soul, cried out to me

I think about those old clothes now
Hear the crisp sound of snaps,
The feel of silk, old cotton, worn denim
As I look through catalogs, online

I still shop at thrift stores, though
Housewares never talk to me

Change

There are things that cannot last
Change does make the present, past
Those that listen to Nature's call
Eroding canyons, leaves of fall
Animals migrate, prey is caught
Our life cycles sometimes short

Clothes and shoes worn to the bare
Our skin and graying, thinning hair
Weight does change, breasts do fall
Our minds do fail, we can't recall
Hearts are broken, then are healed
Death does come, our fate is sealed

Women flow with the present, past
Part of the cycle, our bodies' caste
Instinctively knowing the earth by name
The sun and moon, the tides refrain
Change, like waves of devotion, love
Compromise or loss, we rise above

Like trees that grow from a forest fire
Or children born as elders expire
War's devastation replaced by peace
Our collective conscience does increase
We change, we grow, keep hope alive
For Justice, Harmony, for rights we strive

There are things that cannot last
As we know "This too shall pass"
Our soul's education is what remains
Lessons learned from joys and pains
Each time we incarnate on the Earth
Our stewards role we do rebirth

So let's meditate, to yourself be true
Dispel the fear that makes you blue
The Earth our mother will remain
Empires fall that devalue her name
Things are shifting, the old comes undone
The Age of Aquarius, has begun

Hold love and light to heart, be clear
Regardless of distance, time or fear
The Goddess is not far from shore
She's already knocking at our door
Welcome Change, it comes at last
They who come, make present, past

Fire Is Her War Drum

Mother Nature burns red hot
    Her winds lash out in an angry firestorm
    Beat those drums Sisters, for Mother Earth
    She is all of us, shaking with rage and fury
Her fire is her war drum screaming:
    "Do you think suffocating me with pesticides,
    Smothering my air with toxic waste,
    Poisoning my waters, my life-blood,
    Is without consequences?"
Her fire is her war drum roaring:
    "Do you think I won't notice my parched land,
    When my oceans warm, clog with plastic,
    When my animals starve and die.
    Do you think there are no consequences?"
Her fire is her war drum crying:
    "Do you not hear my groans of agony
    As you cut down my forests, strip my soil,
    As you modify my gifts of milk and honey.
    Do you think there are no consequences?"
Beat those war drums Sisters, for Mother Earth
    She is all of us, shaking with rage and fury,
    Beat those war drums for those we lost,
    Their spirits be blessed, their lives not forgotten.
    Stand up Sisters, fight—Gaia depends on us!

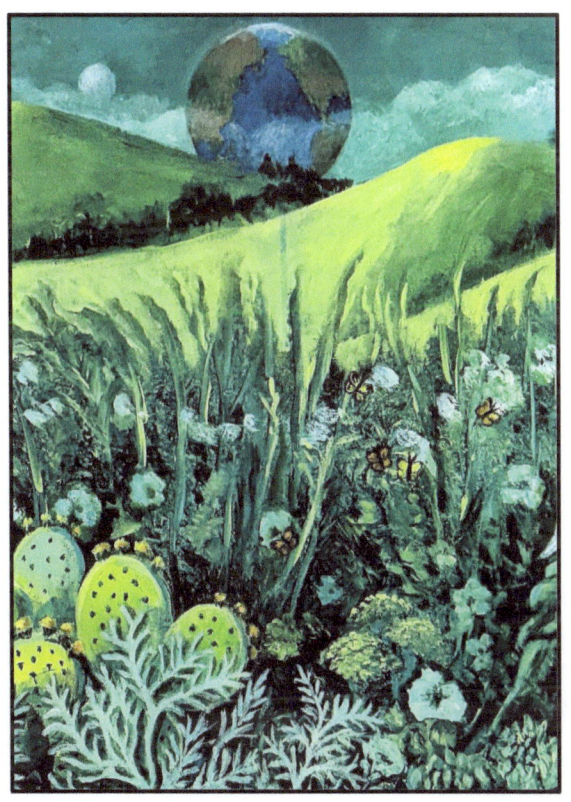

New Earth, acrylic on canvas   *N. Reimer*

In a Perfect World

In a perfect world, there would be no strife
There would be less struggle to just live life
No more war, no rape, poverty or blight
There would be more art, joy, love and light

In a perfect world, Wise Women would reign
Vanquishing lies, greed, hate, and blame
Benevolent leaders with compassion to spare
Children and elders held with utmost care

In a perfect world, soul lessons would enhance
Through ritual, stories, song and dance
No burning, destroying the forests for wood
But, honoring Mother Earth for the highest good

In a perfect world all cultures would share
Unique contributions, with flash and with flair
From one to another appreciation and respect
With time for meditation and peace to reflect

In a perfect world, intuition praised, not denied
All would have homes of safety and pride
Earth's creature, all animals would be seen
Not slaughtered, but held in the highest esteem

In a perfect world, love would be held high
Regardless of gender choice, who, where or why
Each person's integrity and happiness secure
Not killed by laws, based on lies, fears or more

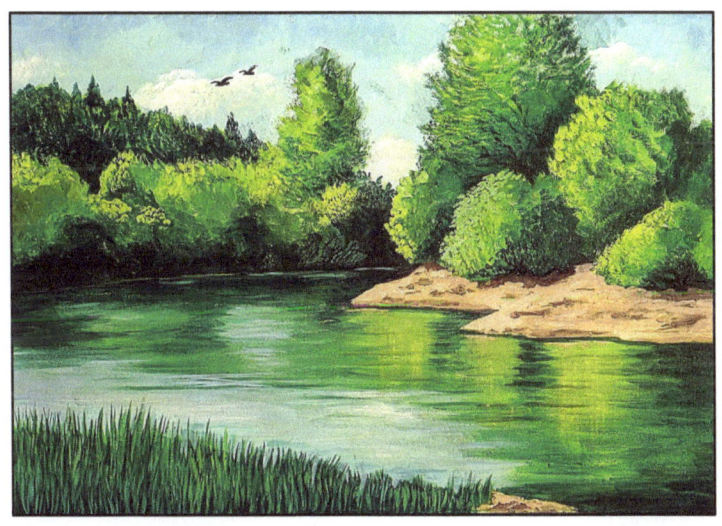

Tranquility, acrylic on canvas   *N. Reimer*

In a perfect world, men would be gentle and wise
Not threatened by women or wish their demise
Women would be conscious, self-loving as well
Education, enlightenment, a universal groundswell

In a perfect world, as the shift on earth nears
The prediction of peace for a thousand years
May heaven on earth heal our land and our seas
Envision our world restored, to beauty and ease

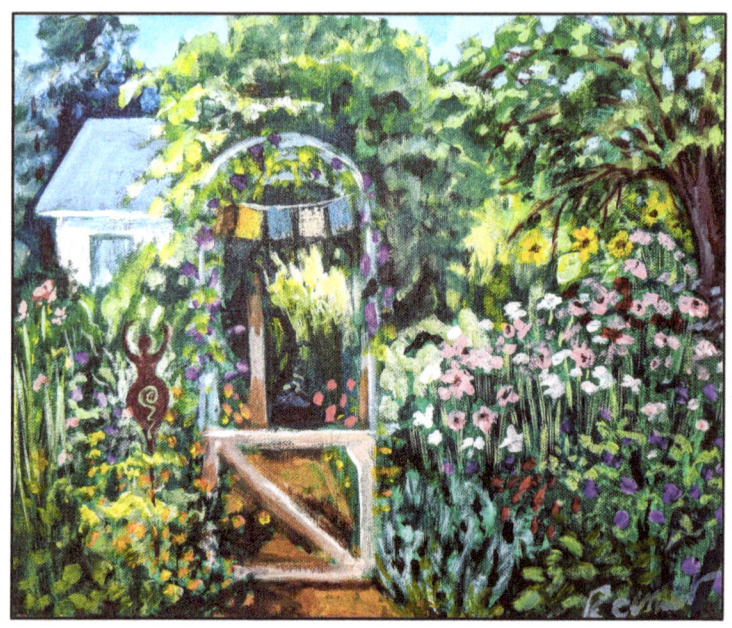

Lucy's Garden II, acrylic on canvas   *N. Reimer*

Dream Garden

In my garden of delight
I dream of her
An enchanting dream of love's tender touch
Drifting fragrance of pink roses and lavender
And the smell of morning dew

When cold winds howl and rain falls
I dream of her anew
Long arms, warm thighs wrapped 'round me
By wood stove fire and candle's flame, I yearn
Breathing her essence in winter's dreams

When spring birds trill in trees at last
I dream of her once more
Where purple iris stretch tall from slumber
And bountiful golden daffodils reach for the sun
I see her in ether's shimmering waves

As summer dreams itself to life
I dream of her again
Till dawn finds her standing tall amidst sunflowers
In my garden of delight, and in plain sight
Her curves, her eyes, her lips—just as I imagined

Many Loves

My first love was tall and sleek
Her teeth like diamonds bright
She'd kiss me every morning
And in the full moonlight

She danced and wrote love poems
Of which she did not boast
We trekked across the country
In her VW coast to coast

My second love was a fairy sprite
A young woman wiry and spry
She wooed me long and arduously
'Til under her spell was I

My third love was a beauty
With a cool personality
A face so stunning gorgeous
I forgot about clarity

We stayed together a long time
Through the thick and thin
I left her some years later
Disagreements made us spin

It was a few a years later when
I'd established a life of worth
I met another on New Years Eve
In my heart, there was rebirth

She was unlike any other
Not intending somcone to meet
A depth of intellect and humor
She swept me off my feet

I loved her with devotion
A passion I'd never known
Finally an intelligent woman
With whom to make a home

Years together thru up and down
Vacationed in summer or fall
We worked and played, danced and sang
We laughed with friends who'd call

One stressful day she said to me
It's over, but we did try
To make a change was hard for us
We'd become friends by and by

Now I'm happy again you see
Resilient to my surprise
Friendship has helped to ease our path
When I look into her eyes

Sometimes I dream of a new love
With spirit, art and poetry
A light-hearted one, sincere and kind
Who finds me her cup of tea

Perhaps someday I'll meet her
Walking along the sandy shore
Or at a party, a gathering
And fall in-love once more

Either way, it will be just fine
Memories line my shelf
I appreciate the time we shared
Each taught me to love myself

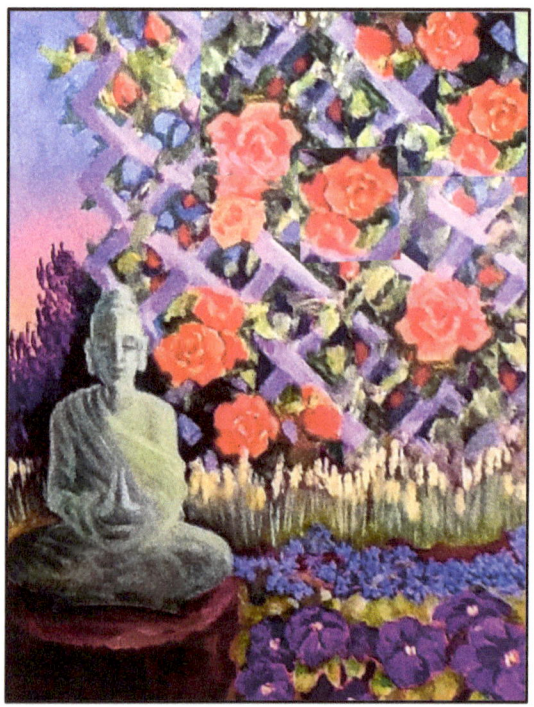

Mediatation Garden, acrylic on canvas   *N. Reimer*

To Be Light-hearted

when the heart is light it floats on air
feels as if there isn't a care

    when the heart is bright it does not hurry
    of right or wrong , it doesn't worry

when the heart is full of love and light
there's no room for fight or flight

    when the heart is love, there's no anger or strife
    compassion is its only life

when the heart's forgiving, it dissolves the grief
soothing feelings, bringing relief

    when the heart is dreaming, it's golden and pink
    a fountain of joy from which to drink

Birthday Song

Alas, the winter's darkness comes in the hour of my age,
as I settle into memories of my past and unknown future.
My mother said "my friends are dying" as she reached the
milestone I stare at now. "Your life spreads out before you,
while my life is behind me," she lamented.

Now, I too have lost so many, some too young to pass.
In spite of the inevitable road we must all walk,
accepting our path to Death's revolving door,
I am grateful, lucky to travel beyond the veil of death,
communicate with the spirits of departed friends—at peace.

By good fortune I still have you, my friends, here and now.
In this year of gratitude, for all the love that's come my way,
I try to feel deserving of it, still shy at praise that comes.
I count my blessings each new dawn, with awe
I greet the day, smile at the early birds singing in the trees.

I rise, alive, well, thankful after so many close calls.
I scoff at the small aches and pains now, while I
put on my jeans and sneakers and refuse to act my age.
I do not allow fear to guide my path, meditate instead
And thank spirit, the universe for gifts big or small.

I wake to find winter's light brighter now, through
bare-leafed trees in the hour of my age, this new age.
Turning over memories, making new ones,
I turn the music up loud so I can sing along and laugh—
"Let's give them something to talk about!"

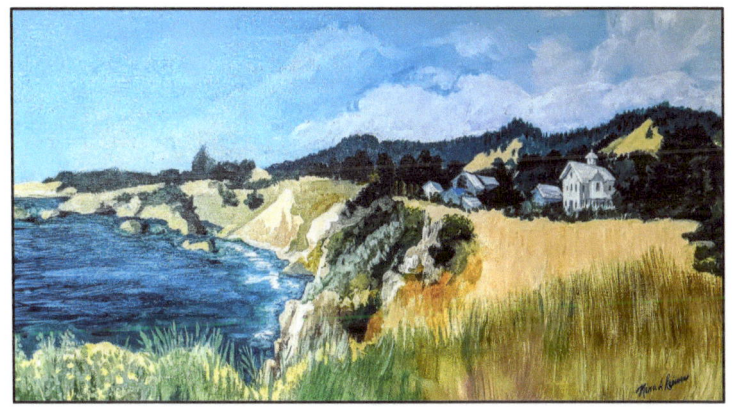

Northern California Summer, oil on canvas   *N. Reimer*

I dance myself into the promise of another day in Eden,
Choosing to live each day awake, as if it is my last,
though I plan to have many more!
Accepting your golden friendship as my right of passage,
I wear your strength, courage and beauty like armor--

And I run toward this age of wisdom, still vibrant,
still hopeful—with arms outstretched in love and joy.

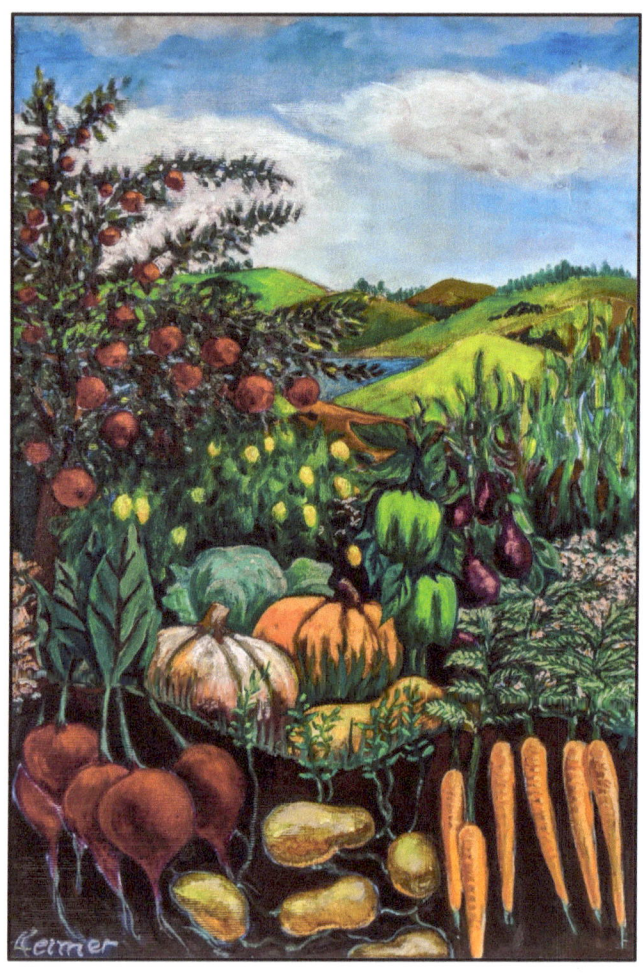

Fall Vegetable Garden, oil on canvas   *N. Reimer*

My Love Is Home

My Love is Beauty, she's old and gray
My love is Wisdom, she laughs all day

    My Love is Growth, she plants and prunes
    My Love is Art, she sings with loons

My Love is Strength, she cooks me soup
My Love is Respect, she stays in the loop

    My Love is Courage, she lights the fire
    My Love is Energy, she holds my desire

My Love is Joy, she smiles in the rain
My Love is Honesty, she accepts her pain

    My Love is Intelligence, she travels the land
    My Love is Affection, she holds my hand

My Love is Respect, she meditates with trees
My Love is Kindness, she speaks like the breeze

    My Loves is Fierceness, she plays the drum
    My Love is Home, hearts joined as one

About the Author/Artist

Ayin Weaver has been creating poetry for several years. In addition, her two novels, *Bleed Through* and *Souls of Viridian* have received 5 star reviews and are available at Amazon and local bookstores. She is currently completing the trilogy with the upcoming third novel.

Artist Nina Ayin Reimer is the original illustrator of the book *Our Bodies, Ourselves* (Simon & Schuster, 1971). Her book *Artist As Healer, Stories of Transforamtion and Healing* is available on Amazon. Her work can also be seen at dollsforthesoul.com or artflare.net.